Packing for FEMA Camp

Mom and Dad Normal Learn About the National Debt, PetroDollars, and the Global Economy

---

A political satire
By F. T. Moore

A Kindle Single by Pergados Press

For bulk print copies, contact Pergados Press at
www.FTMoore.com

For print copies:
ISBN-13: 978-1492902300
ISBN-10: 1492902306

This essay is a work of fiction, and is intended as satire. Any similarity between real people, real places, or real events, is entirely coincidental, or is used fictitiously, and is a product of the author's imagination. References to the workings of the global economy are vastly over-simplified, hopefully to the point of comedic error. But that doesn't mean they don't reveal the Truth, because Truth can only be told through Fiction.

Images courtesy of
http://www.freeimages.co.uk and http://creepyhalloweenphoto.com

The Blog Posts in this essay were first printed at:
http://AuthorFTMoore.wordpress.com

Introduction

When I was studying engineering, there was one concept I just couldn't grasp. I struggled with it, until finally I went to a tutor. My tutor's name was Dinos, and he was Greek. He understood my problem.

"Ahh, yes," Dinos told me, when I explained my difficulty. "This is indeed a hard concept. I struggled with this concept for nine years, until I understood it."

I felt dismayed, that I would have to work on this concept for nine years before I would understand it. But Dinos continued.

"Now that I understand it," he explained, "I can teach it to you in twenty minutes." The moral of Dinos' story was that something that cannot be explained in twenty minutes, is not fully understood by the person who is explaining it.

After engineering school, I went into business. I studied business and economics for nine years, and finally understood it. So here's my twenty minute explanation of global economics, the geo-politics of war, and the national debt. You may not agree with my viewpoint, but as they say at the Harvard Business School:

You got nine economists. You got thirteen opinions.

This series of blog posts explaining "money" was first published on my blog at:
http://AuthorFTMoore.wordpress.com

I hope you enjoy this brief satire.

F T Moore

Part 0. Meet the Normals

om and Dad Normal are Baby Boomers. They live in Bathtub Falls, in a pleasant housing development, on Primrose Lane. They always vote, although Mom votes Democrat and Dad votes Republican so they cancel each other out. Their children are grown. Mom and Dad are just entering their late fifties/early sixties, and they hoped to be planning retirement now, but things don't look as good as they hoped. Mom lost her job a few years ago, and hasn't been able

Mom and Dad Normal

to get a new one, so they aren't saving any more. They hope Dad will keep working and never retire. They put their savings into their 401Ks at work, but lo and behold, that didn't add up to much money after all.

Recently, Mom and Dad learned that the NSA is capturing all the data from their phone calls and emails and storing it in a big database. They thought that was no problem, because they have nothing to hide. Also, they want to be safe, and the world is a dangerous place. Although Mom and Dad are aware that their risk of being killed by a terrorist is less than their risk of falling in the bathtub, they worry anyway. They are so glad that Homeland Security is keeping them safe.

Dad Normal's name is George. George has a degree in engineering. He works for a defense contractor, Marietta-Northrup-Hughes-Root Systems Science Corporation. George has held the same job his entire life. All of his retirement savings are in his 401K plan at the office.

Mom Normal's name is Linda. Linda worked as a secretary at the same company as George, but she was laid off in 2008 and has not gone back to work.

Mom and Dad Normal's 25-year-old son, Abe Normal, lives in their basement because he works at BoxMart and doesn't make a living wage. Abe has a degree in Criminal Justice from State College and is paying off his student loans. Mom and Dad are co-signers on those loans, so they let him live in the basement rent-free. He has his own mini-bar down there and a private entrance.

Their 24-year-old daughter, Sue B. Normal , is a middle school teacher. She teaches eighth grade social studies. Sue B. has been learning about the risks of terrorism, in her class to arm schoolteachers. As she learns things, she explains them to Mom and Dad.

They have a neighbor, Buck Stopshere, who is trying to get Dad to join the Tea Party.

Mom and Dad Normal learn new things every day. They are interested and curious about their world, and that's why they watch Mainstream Media News at 11 pm, every night.

A while ago, Mom and Dad Normal watched President Barack Obama on the Jay Leno show. The President said, specifically, that the U.S. does not do any domestic spying. This put Mom and Dad's worries to rest. Then Michael Hayden, former NSA director, explained to them that people who concern themselves with domestic spying are domestic terrorists, who live in their parent's basements and waste their lives on the Internet.

They immediately ran to the basement to check on their son, Abe, but he was sleeping. He had his backpack open, so they looked inside to see if there was a pressure cooker in there. Finding nothing but an empty Dorito's bag, they felt calmer and went to bed.

The next morning, they awoke to the news that Senator McCain wanted the U.S. to punish Russia for refusing to extradite that Traitor-Boy, Edward Snowden. They also were encouraged to hear that the NSA spying program successfully listened in on a coven of Al Qaeda operatives, who made a big conference call. All the BigShots in Al Qaeda were on the call, and they laid out all their plans, their organization structure, and their command structure. They identified a Big Plot in the future. Mom and Dad were giggly-happy to hear that President Obama responded by closing 20 U.S. embassies. They didn't want another Benghazi in their future.

Just then, Abe came up from the basement, in his bare feet, smelling like he needed a shower. He scratched his belly and yawned, as the news droned on.

"Funny," Abe said, through his sleepy yawn, "you'd think Al Qaeda would know not to use telephones now, after Snowden told them about the NSA. They never used them before."

http://www.thedailybeast.com/articles/2013/08/07/al-qaeda-conference-call-intercepted-by-u-s-officials-sparked-alerts.html

Then Abe went back to bed.

Dad Normal looked up from his Washington Post. Across the breakfast table to Mom, he said, "Is Benghazi the capital of Libya?"

"No," Mom said. "It's Tripoli."

http://abcnews.go.com/blogs/politics/2011/09/american-flag-raised-over-u-s-embassy-in-tripoli/

"Huh," Dad said. "I wonder why there was an American embassy there."

http://www.mcclatchydc.com/2012/11/12/174455/libyans-diplomats-cias-benghazi.html

And the sleep goes on.

Part 1: Mom and Dad Normal Learn About Bankers

Mom and Dad Normal are having budget problems. Dad says their monthly credit card bill – the one they pay off fully each month – has doubled in the last five years. They put food, gas for their cars, haircuts, clothes, household items, and entertainment on that card. Mom says they aren't buying any more or less than they bought five years ago. Has inflation been twenty percent a year for the last five years, Dad says?

This is what wampum looks like

Their 25-year-old son, Abe, comes up from the basement where he's been living since he graduated from college. He says, "I saw a tv show about that. It's called Quantitative Easing."

"Quantitative Easing?" says Mom. "What's that?"

Sue B. Normal, their school teacher daughter, says "Oh, that's the word the Federal Reserve uses to mean inflation, because they can't call it inflation any more. If they called it inflation, they'd have to raise payments on Social Security checks to match it."

Dad Normal lays down his Wall Street Journal. "What are you talking about?" he asks Sue.

And so Sue B. Normal explains to Mom and Dad what money is. And here's the conversation:

Where Bankers Come From, by Sue B. Normal

In the beginning of the world, people exchanged favors to help each other out. But as societies got bigger, and people developed desires to have more things, primitive tribes came up with the idea to pick something of value to use as a measurement of trade. In some lands, a rock of a certain size or shape became the designated measuring value. In Native America, some tribes used "wampum." Wampum was a set of beads, in strings of varying lengths. The point of wampum was to assign units of value, so that people could make trades of goods and skills that would make everyone feel they had traded fairly and equitably. It was a measurement system for value. People like to think trades are fair, and so it made everybody happy when the Wampum System was invented. While every tribe and nation developed its own scale for measuring value, most nations ultimately set up a system of money, so that the bartering of labor and goods could be perceived to be equitable.

When one person in the tribe had a lot to offer, in terms of skills, that person may end up with a BIG pile of wampum. If they already had everything they needed, they might not have anything to spend their wampum on. They might be too busy collecting more wampum, by giving out their services, for example. So that person would have a pile of wampum sitting in their teepee. Teepees are small, and they don't have locks on the doors, but nobody in Native American society ever stole the wampum. It would be disgraceful. However, while theft was socially unacceptable, somebody in the tribe would often come to a Wampum Maker and ask to borrow.

"I will gladly pay you back on Tuesday, for a loan of wampum today," they would say. The Wampum Makers always said yes, because that was polite.

Over time, the Wampum Makers noticed that their piles of wampum were getting smaller, because all the people who borrowed the wampum, never paid it back.

Eventually the Wampum Maker would seek out another member of the tribe, and ask that person to take care of their wampum for them, by burying it along the side of the river bank. These people were called Bankers. Banking would be an important service, because the Wampum Maker was too busy performing more important services. He didn't have time to safeguard his old wampum while he was busy getting new wampum. So the Bankers and the Wampum Makers formed a pact. The Wampum Makers would loan all their money to the Bankers, and the Bankers promised to keep it safe and return it whenever the Wampum Makers asked for it.

In any society, there are some members who don't have much skill to give as barter. These people may be old, infirm, or terminally stupid. Or, they may be members of the military, and therefore not available to perform services within the tribe because they are busy fighting enemies. So these people would go to the Tribal Chief, and say, "Can you give us some wampum, because we don't have any?"

The Tribal Chief would look around the tribe, and see who had extra wampum. He would go to that person and say, "Can you give some wampum to these poor people? And also, can you give wampum to me, so I can pay my Brave Warriors?"

The Wampum Maker remembered what happened when he loaned wampum to people before. He knew if he gave it away, he would soon have none left for himself. So he would say: "I would, but I can't, because I gave it to the Banker and he hid it."

Then the Tribal Chief would go to the Banker. "Banker, can you give me, and also these poor people, some wampum?"

The Banker would say: "How much will you pay me to do it?"

Then the Chief would say, "I will give you back your original wampum, plus 10% more, but I will need some time to pay."

The Banker, realizing that he can give the original rich man all of his wampum back, plus skim 5% off for himself and 5% more for the Wampum Maker says to the Chief, "Okay, I'll give you some money."

And this is the Bottom Line of the relationship between the Federal Reserve (the Banker), the President of the United States (the Tribal Chief), the elite class of the 0.1% (the Wampum Makers), and the rest of the people in the World.

Next: Mom and Dad Normal Learn How the Federal Reserve Works

Part 2: Mom and Dad Normal Learn About the Federal Reserve Bank

"**W**ait," Mom Normal says to her school teacher daughter. "Sue, you said the Tribal Chief promised to pay the Banker 10% more than he borrowed. Where does the Tribal Chief get the wampum to repay the Banker?"

The Banker of the Federal Reserve

"Ahh, Mom, you are so sharp," says Sue. "That is exactly the right question. And it is the crux of the issue of Class Warfare in the world today. So let's look at that in detail.

How the Federal Reserve Works, by Sue B. Normal

Now, the Tribal Chief gets wampum by asking all the members of the tribe to pay a fee, called "tax." The plan is that the Tribal Chief will repay the Banker by sending him the tax money. Over time, this will pay back the amount borrowed, plus interest. So the Chief goes around to all the tribe members and collects the tax. But when he counts up the wampum from the tax, he has a problem: all the poor people who received the wampum from the government. There's no point collecting tax from them, because they only have the wampum the Chief gave them. So the Chief collects the tax from the other tribe members, the ones who have enough wampum from their daily work, but not too much extra wampum that they could afford to give any of it to the Banker to save. They grumble about it, but they hand their wampum over. These people, who have enough wampum for themselves, but not enough extra to hide in the River Bank, are called The Middle People. So all the people in the tribe are: The Wampum Makers, the Bankers, the Poor People, and the Middle People.

The Tribal Chief counts all the Tax Wampum, and he figures out how many years it will take to pay back the Banker what he owes. Then he sets the Rate on his Tribal Treasury Bonds to match his calculation. All is well. Everyone will be happy with this Wampum System. The Chief will pay the Wampum Makers their wampum back over time, and he will use this borrowed wampum to run the tribe.

Then a Big War comes. The Chief needs the warriors to go fight enemies. So the regular people who had just enough wampum to get by, have to stop working, so they can go join the Army. Now there are more people in the Army who are users of wampum. The Chief has to pay them with the Tax Wampum. There aren't enough people left to pay taxes. So the Chief goes to the Wampum Maker and asks him to pay tax.

The Wampum Maker squawks: Wait a minute. Hold on. You are asking me to pay tax, so you can repay me for the loan of my own wampum? What is this? Socialism? The problem here is that you have too many poor people. Go away, or I will call my Loan, and you will not have years to pay me back. I will take my Wampum and move away from your Tribe, to a different country. Then you will no longer be Chief of the Tribe.

Quickly, the Chief backs off. He needs years to pay back the loan from the Banker, and besides that, he has more Big Wars coming, so he had in mind that he was going to ask for another loan. He recognizes his mistake in approaching the Wampum Makers and asking them to pay tax. Tax, he reminds himself, is only for the Middle People. But the Chief is out of Wampum. What can he do?

The Chief goes to the Banker again. He says to the Banker, can I have some more wampum, so I can pay you back my loan?

The Banker looks in the hole, where he stored the wampum, and he sees that there is very little wampum in there, because the Chief hasn't paid him back for the first loan. "If I give you another loan, how much will you pay me for this new wampum?" says the Banker.

This time, the Chief says, I will pay you 15%, plus all your wampum back.

The Banker smiles. He knows there is very little wampum in the Vault. But the Chief doesn't know. So he says, "Chief, wait here. I will be right back."

The Banker calls a meeting of all the Wampum Makers from all the Tribes all over the world. They meet at a forest called Bretton Woods. He tells the Wampum Makers of the world all about the problem: the hole is nearly empty, but the Chief wants another loan. The Wampum Makers look at each other. What should they do?

"There needs to be more Wampum in the world, but there isn't enough to take care of everybody," says the Banker.

"That's ridiculous," says the Wampum Maker who owns railroads. "We can always just change the value of wampum to make there be enough for everybody. It's not necessary to make the value of wampum always stay the same."

Then the other Wampum Makers put their heads together. How can they solve this problem? "Wait," says the Wampum Maker who owns the coal mines. "We can't just change the value of the wampum to make it fit. That would cause all of our wampum to be less valuable. It would be like diluting our stock."

WampumMakers, putting their heads together to solve the problem of too little wampum in the world

"You're right," said the Wampum Maker who owned the steel mills. "We cannot take any action that would lower the value of our own wealth. Something has to be done that will multiply our wealth, not divide it. We cannot allow the value of wampum to float."

All the Wampum Makers agreed. No action could be taken that would dilute the value of their existing wealth.

Then the Witch Doctor, who was one of the Wampum Makers, spoke up: "Does the Chief know the hole is empty?"

"No," says the Banker.

"Then give him this piece of Magic Straw, which is called a Promissory Note. Tell him you have all the Wampum in the world hidden in a hole called Fort Knox, and this piece of Straw is a representation of that Wampum. Tell him he can trade these pieces of Straw, and turn them in for Wampum at any time. Tell him all he has to do is present his Straw at the Wampum Window, and it will be redeemed for Wampum."

The other Wampum Makers nodded. "But what about the problem of needing more?" they said.

"Banker," the Witch Doctor said, "give out 100 pieces of Straw for every piece of Wampum left in the Vault. When you get to 100 pieces of Straw for every 1 piece of Wampum, stop making loans. That will be enough."

The Banker was excited. These wonderful, benevolent Wampum Makers had just turned Straw into Wampum. Now there would be one hundred times more Wampum in the world. What fine, benevolent Human Beings these Wampum Makers were.

The Banker nodded, and he rushed to tell the Chief that his new loans were approved.

All the Wampum Makers were happy. This system was going to work. Every piece of Straw was now a loan. From THEM. Now, every Tribal Chief would owe the Wampum Makers 100 Times more Wampum than the Wampum Makers ever had to loan. They would be rich forever, through all the generations in the world. And it was all because of this brilliant Witch Doctor's wonderful idea. They called him The Economist, and they patted him on the back and pinky-swore their allegiance to his Cult. "Never explain," their motto became, and they wrote it on their family crests, to remind them that they must never tell the secret of the Empty Vault and how they made it appear to be full again.

Then the Wampum Makers got old and died. Their children, the Spoons, inherited all their Wampum. But their Wampum was all gone, because it had been loaned to the Chief, to give to the Poor People and the Warriors. All the Spoons had left were the Promises from the Banker to give their wampum back from the Tax Wampum, over time. How could they spend Promises? They asked the Witch Doctor.

And so the Witch Doctor built a Trade School on the River Bank in Cambridge, Massachusetts, called Harvard Business School. There the Spoons would go, and send their children, to learn the Shell Game, which would allow them to spend their Empty Promises. And they all learned the creed: Never, never, never explain where their wampum came from.

Next: How did the Empty Promises turn into Black Gold?

Part 3: How did the Empty Promises turn into Black Gold?

"Sue," said Mom Normal. "I don't understand why anybody would loan America money in exchange for empty air. That doesn't make sense."

"You're right, Mom," said Sue. "It's completely, unbelievably simple-minded. But the whole world is doing it. Everybody in the world uses the Dollar as their reserve currency. That means all the other countries promised to keep their savings in U.S. Treasury Bonds. So they are all loaning America money."

A Break from the Rules of the Club would be poison to the Wampum System

Abe yawned and scratched his belly. "Everybody except Syria, Iran, Libya, Iraq, Lebanon, Somalia, and Iran."

"That's an odd list of countries," Dad said. "Those are the countries General Wesley Clark identified as the ones the U.S. decided to go to war with ten days after the 9/11 attacks, didn't he? Those countries don't lend money to the United States, but everybody else does?"

"Sharia Law," Abe said. "Didn't want to get involved in usury."

http://libertycrier.com/general-wesley-clark-wars-planned-seven-countries-five-years-syria-included/

"Why would countries lend money to the U.S?" Mom asked. "We're the rich nation. Nobody has to lend money to us."

"We were the rich nation," Sue said. "At one time. But times have changed."

How American Banksters Created a Ponzi Scheme, by Sue B. Normal

Every few days, the Chief kept coming back to the Banker, asking for another loan. He had his Magic Straw, and he was distributing it like crazy. In fact, there was so much Straw being loaned to so many people, that some people were becoming Wampum Makers themselves! New wealth creators were arising, people who were not members of the Cult of the Spoons.

Regular Poor People and Middle People were rising from their poverty, and becoming new Wampum Makers themselves. These people were called the Nouveau Riche, because they liked to use their Wampum to jet off to Paris in their private planes. It was scandalous! The Nouveau Riche made exhibits of themselves, calling attention to their wealth, and allowing the Middle People to see how rich they were.

The Spoons buzzed with disgust. These Pirates were breaking the first rule of Money Club, which is:

Never Talk About Money Club.

The Spoons learned from the cradle, from their Wet Nurse's breast, this important rule. They learned it at their Father's knee and their Mother's diamond apron.

Never Talk About Money Club.

The Spoons realized this was getting to be a dangerous situation. It was a threat to their God-given identity, as the inherited wealthy. After all, said the Spoons to each other, if God didn't want us to be rich, we wouldn't have been born with spoons in our mouths. And it had to be true, because they saw that many of the Nouveau Riche got rich from Crime Activities, like diamond smuggling, gun running, moonshine, gambling casinos, and drug dealing. Some of the Nouveau Riche got rich from selling things to the Tribal Chief, so he could make bigger wars. And some of the Nouveau Riche got rich from selling Oil. Mostly, there was something fishy about how they got Nouveau Riche, so they generally didn't hang around a lot with the Bankers. All of the Nouveau Riche had Magic Straw, not real Wampum. They knew a little bit about real Wampum, and some of them bought some of it, but mostly, the Nouveau Riche thought it was okay to keep their money in Magic Straw.

They weren't allowed into the club, where the Cult of the Spoons met, so they didn't really understand the difference between Magic Straw and Wampum. But they were a little bit confused about how Magic Straw worked, because they didn't know they had to go to the Trade School to learn about the Federal Reserve. So these Nouveau Riche Pirates didn't keep their Magic Straw in the Bank, like obedient Spoons did. They kept going to the Wampum Window, and trying to get Wampum to hide in a different hole, outside of the hole at Fort Knox. One crazy New Pirate, whose name was Qaddafi, hid his gold in Africa, and tried to get all the African people to use Gold Dinars instead of Promises made of Magic Straw! It was unthinkable! Unallowable! Unbearable! Intolerable!

This made the members of the Cult of the Spoon nervous. "The rules of the cult cannot be broken," they said. "All the Nouveau Riche must put their wampum into the Bank. If there is a crack in the system, the system will break apart." They called the Witch Doctor and he had a talk with the Banker.

"What are we going to do if these new Wampum Makers won't put their wampum in the vault?" the Spoons asked the Witch Doctor and the Banker. "All wampum has to go through the Vault. It's the only way that Straw can turn into 100 X Wampum. All the New Rich People must buy into the Federal Reserve, and keep their Wampum safely in the Vault. Our personal fortunes are tied to repayment of our loans to the Tribal Treasury, six generations ago. It's how we stay unspeakably wealthy. We can't allow these Nouveau Riche to keep their Magic Straws out of the Banking System!"

"We're going to have to get some help from the Tribal Chief," said the Witch Doctor. "Banker, you must tell the Chief that we do not need to have limits on our American Exceptionalism. It should not just be the Spoons who are rich. We can make room for all the New Rich Capitalists who are contributing so productively to our nation. As long as all capital trade is conducted in Magic Straw, there should be no need to tie the Magic Straw to physical Wampum. Then the Chief will get everybody to keep putting all their Straw in the Bank. We do not need any new rich people having any physical Wampum-Gold. It's not necessary. It limits our growth as a nation."

"Maybe," said the group of Spoons, "the problem is that we haven't given the Tribal Chiefs any money for themselves. Maybe our system needs to employ these people, so that they understand where their bread is buttered."

But other Spoons said, "That would be very dangerous. It may require us to talk about money. And we never talk about money."

So the Spoons rejected the idea of employing the Tribal Chiefs. Instead, they employed some Middle People called Lobbyists. And they said, "Don't tell us how you solve this problem. We will give you some Money, and you make the problem go away. But don't tell us how you made it go away because we . . ."

Never Talk About Money

And now, all the people in the world were made up of:

The Spoons. The Nouveau Riche Pirates. The Middle People. The Poor People. The Set of World Tribal Chiefs. and The Lobbyists

The next time the Chief came to the Banker for a loan, the Banker said:

"Chief, there are many people out there who want to get more and more wampum. This is a problem because there is not enough wampum to pay all the people who come to the wampum window. These are evil speculators, who want to hoard the wampum all for themselves and not put it to work driving the forces of our Capitalist System. But I believe we should not yield to such evil speculators. I believe we should take the Tribe off the wampum-standard. Then those bad people who are asking for their wampum back cannot interfere with our American Exceptionalism."

The Chief did not know that the Banker was tricking him. The Chief did not know that the Promises from the bank had physical limits, and that untying the Straw from the Wampum was going to change everything. The Chief did not know that the Banker was doing something that would tie the Bank economy to the Underground Cash economy, cutting it off forever from physical Gold. The Chief did not know that allowing Cash to flow freely, without a physical tie to solid Gold-Wampum, was going to allow the Mobsters who sold drugs and diamonds and guns a free pass to launder their money through the staid and sturdy national banking system.

And so the Chief nodded. He was happy. It was going to work! The Banker was going to give him another loan! Hurray! Sure, the Chief says, Let's go off the Wampum-Standard. Where do I sign?

And so in 1971, Richard Nixon turned the Federal Reserve from a Service Window for the Spoons into a full-fledged money-laundering Bankster system. And the Exceptional American Tribe has been borrowing Air ever since.

"Sue," Dad said. "I'm starting to think this story is an Allegory. What are you saying, in real life?"

"Well, Dad," said Sue, "At the end of World War II, all 40 of the Allied nations were in economic chaos. The war had taken a big toll, and the United States of America was the conquering hero. The Allied nations all sent delegates to a conference in New Hampshire, called Bretton Woods. The Allies were the winners of the war, but they didn't feel like winners, because their economies were devastated. The United States of America, however, was doing well. War manufacturing stimulated the economy, and it was strong.

Up until then, countries traded goods and services by physically sending gold to even up their trade deficits. If one country bought more than it sold, it would have to make up the difference by sending a ship full of gold to the nation it owed. This was the only way to figure out a trade imbalance, because the currency of one nation could not be compared to the currency of another. Nations' economies were unstable, so other countries would not accept payment in anything but gold. This is why there are so many sunken pirate ships in the ocean.

But after the war, nobody wanted to keep fighting off pirates. Pirates were all over the ocean, attacking ships, and stealing gold. So the United States proposed that America keep all the gold in the world in Fort Knox. Then everybody could buy Dollars, which would all be worth exactly $35 per ounce of gold. It would be a currency that didn't fluctuate. Everybody would be safe from the Pirates.

This sounded like a good deal at the time, considering that people had just seen Germany get hit by an inflation that made all their currency worthless. So all the countries signed a deal. All the gold would physically be stored in the United States, and other nations would hold U.S. Treasury Bonds (that is, I O Us from the United States of America) for their portion of the gold.

From 1945 until 1971, this system allowed countries all over the world to loan money to the United States, by buying U.S. Treasury Bonds, which were consistently pegged to a physical ounce of gold, at $35 per ounce. The gold was stored in the vault at Fort Knox.

And then one day the Bankster let the Tribal Chief in on a secret. There wasn't enough gold in there."

"So Richard M. Nixon took the Dollar off the Gold Standard," Mom guessed.

"But don't worry," said Big Brother. "He put it on the Oil Standard instead."

Next: The Impact of the Petro-Dollar on Acts of War

Part 4: The Impact of the Petro-Dollar on the Act of War

"I'm really glad America was able to help everybody in the world get back on their feet after World War II," Mom Normal said to her family. "That was a great thing, that we agreed to keep everybody's gold safe for them, so they wouldn't have to worry about pirates stealing it."

"Yes," said Dad Normal. "Then all the other countries could put their savings into U.S. Treasury Bonds, which are the safest investment in the world."

"You do know that buying a U.S. Bond is like loaning money to America, don't you?" Sue asked. "So nations all over the world have their savings in loans to the US Government."

"Sure," said Dad. "That makes sense. Those other countries can feel good about their savings, because America is Exceptional."

OPEC and the Petro-Dollar, by Sue B. Normal

Richard Nixon, Tribal Chief of America in 1971, was not a stupid man. As much as he knew he had to disconnect the U.S. Dollar from the gold in Fort Knox, because the vault didn't have enough gold in it, he also knew this was a BIG problem. Yeah, yeah, yeah, those TV pundits were going to tell the world it didn't matter, but hell-in-a-hand-basket, it *did* matter. It mattered a whole lot. Because the reason the gold was all gone was that America was running a trade deficit.

America was buying more goods than it was selling. It was that simple. Other countries were using their national savings to buy U.S. Treasury Debt; that is, they were loaning money to the USA. And the USA was spending it all, without producing enough goods to pay it back.

Once the Chief closed the wampum window, the dollar began to free fall. Inflation was up. Unemployment was up. Those two are supposed to run opposite each other, but now they weren't. Something had to be done. The US Dollar could not be a "fiat currency." It was too important for the global economy. If the Dollar operated without the backing of Gold, the USA risked its position in world dominance.

So Henry Kissinger, Personal Witch Doctor Assigned to the Tribal Chief, thought of something. He went to Saudi Arabia. He offered them United States military protection of their oil fields in return for making Black Gold (Oil) the backing for the U.S. Dollar. If the Saudi leaders would agree to accept only U.S. Dollars to buy oil, then the U.S. would protect the oil fields militarily and also protect the price of oil in the market. Every country that wanted OPEC oil would have to pay for it in U.S. Dollars. Because oil was so important for a nation to grow, each country started keeping its "reserve" money in U.S. Treasury Bonds. That meant the nations of the world would continue to loan money to America by buying U.S. Dollars through the purchase of Treasury Bonds. So the price of oil went up, and all the countries of the world could only buy oil through their purchase of U.S. Debt.

What did this mean, in the end? In the end of the end, it meant the United States of America could print money with nothing to back it. No other country could do that, because they all had to buy their oil by purchasing U.S. Treasury Bonds. Dollars became themselves the wampum of value. It meant that the Banksters of the Federal Reserve could print money, loan it to the U.S.Treasury, and keep doing that without limit. The debt ceiling could always be raised. There was no limit to how much money could be printed. There was nothing to physically stop the printing of more money. The word for "The U.S. Treasury is printing more money" became "Quantitative Easing."

And why could the Banksters print more money? Because all they really had to do was raise the price of oil. It was floating value. Abracadabra. Magic Straw turned into Black Gold. This is why we say "Float a Bond Issue."

"Whoa, there, Sue B." said Dad Normal. "OPEC decides the price of oil. Not the U.S.Treasury or the Federal Reserve."

"Sorry, Dad," said Sue. "The Banksters decide. You see, nations everywhere must build up a trade surplus, by selling more things to the USA than they buy. It's necessary, in order for them to get oil. If they can't get oil, they can't develop their economy. The only way for them to get oil is to have some dollars to buy it with. They can only get dollars by having some savings to buy U.S. Treasury Bonds. It's not as complicated as it sounds. The system's rigged so that the USA runs a constant trade deficit, borrows money from all the other countries who want oil, and they all have to have savings while the USA lives on credit."

"Sweet deal," Abe inserted. "Sweet, sweet deal for the USA."

"Sweet until the other nations get sick of it, and vomit it up," said Dad.

"Sweet until it's over," piped in Mom.

"Bingo," said Sue. "Like every Ponzi scheme, it's going great until the day some crazy oil-producing country decides it's going to sell oil to people who don't have any U.S. Dollars. The Number One Export of the United States, since the advent of the Petrodollar is what?"

"Debt," said Abe.

"You got it," Sue told him. "The US Exports Dollars in the form of government bonds, which are loans to the US Treasury. And in the year 2000, Mr. Saddam Hussein made the mistake of thinking he was going to cleverly bust out of the mold. He tried to make a deal to sell his oil for Euros, instead of dollars."

"Blam. Gotta slam that move into the ground." Said Abe, smacking his hand on his knee.

"You betcha, as we say in Alaska. Why do you think we call it Wall Street?"

"Because it's where Humpty Dumpty sat!" shouted Abe.

Next: What happens when the PetroDollar currency collapses.

Part 5: What happens when the PetroDollar currency collapses.

"So let me get this straight," Dad Normal said. "The U.S. Dollar is not backed by gold, but it is backed by oil, is that what you're saying?"

"In the sense that you mostly have to have U.S. Dollars to buy oil," said his schoolteacher daughter, Sue. "All over the world, people can only buy oil with U.S. Dollars. Venezuela made a few agreements to let Latin American countries barter with them for oil. OPEC, however, still requires payment in US Dollars. Even Russia, the world's second largest oil producer, requires payment in US Dollars. The U S Dollar is the world's global reserve currency. That means nations keep their savings in U S Treasury Bonds, thereby loaning money to America."

PetroDollars in All Their Glory

"But I don't get it," Mom Normal interjected. "Why would Russia agree to do that? Why would Middle East countries agree to do it? Those countries hate us! Why would they keep loaning us money?"

"More importantly," Abe added, swigging his morning breakfast Red Bull, "why do all those other countries have money to loan, while we're a country with this mega-trillion dollar debt?"

"Well," said Sue, getting out her flipchart easel and hoisting her pad of flipchart paper on top, "there is a difference between deciding to do something, and deciding to stop doing something. The entire world started buying oil with U.S. Dollars back when the Dollar was backed by gold, in 1944. That continued by fiat, when the currency went off the gold standard, and OPEC demanded that the US Dollar payments continue. Times have changed. The world demand for oil has changed. The geopolitics of the world has changed. It looked like a good idea at the end of World War II, when the U S economy was strong relative to the rest of the world. That's when currency exchanges effectively based themselves on a global standard, the U S Dollar. It doesn't look like such a good idea now, now that the US exports so much less than it imports.

"We're basically almost 70 years into a global plan to price trade in U S Dollars. National treasuries all over the world are chock full of United States Government

Bonds, which are debt. So what will happen if those people who are holding the debt, all decide to stop the train. What if Russia says, *in the future, I will accept payments only in Russian rubles for my oil?*"

Abe raised his hand. "Oooh, oooh, oooh," he grunted, while stamping his feet up and down.

Sue called on him.

"It depends on how much it happens, and how confident the buyers are in the Russian ruble. If a big oil producer like Russia does it, people will decide whether they want the debt of Russia, or the debt of America. If countries need rubles to buy oil, they have to buy rubles by buying the debt of Russia."

"Whoa," said Dad. "Like *that* would happen." Dad and Mom both chuckle.

"Ha, ha," laughed Mom. "Nobody would buy the debt of Russia. That would be stoopit!"

Sue nodded. "Exactly. This system was in place since 1944. So, you see, other countries have to feel comfortable that the debt they are buying is solid debt, that they will be able to get their money back. So they keep buying U S Dollars, because they have confidence in the American economy. Who would buy the debt of Greece? Or of Spain?"

Abe raised his hand again. "Why can't countries buy oil in their own currency? Why do they have to change their currency into the currency of another country?"

"Oh, I get that," Dad told Abe. "Because the seller of the oil wants to be confident that the currency is sound."

"We're back to confidence in the soundness of the currency again," added Mom.

"There's that word. Confidence. And what puts the Con in Confidence?" Sue asked.

"Public perception," Abe answered. "Worldwide public perception."

"So what did the U S Treasury Secretary, Henry Paulson, think, on that night in 2008 when he realized Lehman Brothers was bankrupt and the U S economy ran out of money?" asked Sue.

"He thought, OMG, the Tribal Chiefs of the world are going to look in the hole and realize there's no wampum in there. Then they're all going to go crazy and declare war on the Banksters and the Banksters are going to be pummeled into oblivion and disappear from the face of the earth. And I'm a BANKSTER. That's what he thought."

"Do you think he considered what would happen to the poor people? All those people who depended on wampum to buy food and shelter? Do you think he worried about whether or not there would still be PopTarts on WalMart shelves?"

"What? The poor people? Well, yes, he thought about the poor people. If you 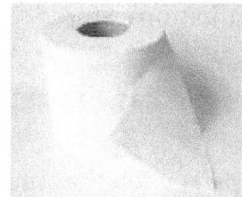 asked him, he would say he did it for the poor people. But one could contend that he's never met one, to think like that. No, the poor people don't need wampum. The poor people operate their economy on Magic Straw, and if they did not have magic straw, they would use toilet paper, just as well. If they have no bread, let them eat cake, the Banksters said."

"The important people aren't poor," Mom added. "The important people are the ones who put that money in the hole. They are the Wampum Makers. The Banksters worry about the Wampum Makers, not the Poor People. So all the Bankster could think about was: where can I get some wampum to push into that hole. Fast."

"Hold it," Dad interrupted. "The Wampum Makers. Didn't they give that money to the United States of America in the beginning? Back when there was no country, and a few patriots were trying to start a revolution? The new government needed gold, and the only place to get it was from the Pirates, right?"

"Yeah, yeah, I get it," added Abe. "The original gold came from the Pirates/Wampum Makers. And then over time, the Federal Reserve started creating money out of Thin Air. "

"So when the Banker needed more money, where did he get it?" Sue asked.

"He had the Federal Reserve print some," answered Dad.

"And when the Federal Reserve prints money, to stuff into the hole of the Banks, that means the banks can lend out 100 times more than actually exists. Creating a new $700 Billion by the Federal Reserve, becomes $70 Trillion circulating in the economy," Mom figured out.

"In the world of digital electronic wampum," Dad added.

"And where is this world?" Sue asked.

"It's Wally World!" shouted Abe, pleased with his powers of observation.

"It's in the mind's eye!" said Mom.

"It's in public perception," nodded Dad.

"Exactly," Sue affirmed. "The world monetary system is Pretend-Bizzarro World. It exists as a myth, which must be protected. It's Santa Claus. As long as everybody keeps believing, those gifts show up under the tree on Christmas morning. But as soon as you stop believing, the magic ends."

"So Russia can't switch to rubles for their oil pricing until the whole world believes that the ruble is a stable currency."

"And no one can risk selling their U S Bonds in any great quantity, because that in itself would de-stabilize the Dollar, which would make all their nation's stores of Dollars worthless."

"The world is between a rock and a hard place. The whole world has a vested interest in keeping the dollar strong."

"No," said Sue. "The whole world has a stake in keeping the *perception* that the dollar is strong. It doesn't matter what is real. It just matters that a whole lot of people don't show up at the Wampum Window asking for Cash. And why is that, Big Brother?"

And Abe answered, "Because the Cash isn't there. Only 1 Magic Straw out of 100 is backed by Oil, Black Gold."

"And the key," offered Dad, "is to make sure no more than 1 out of 100 Petro-dollars is ever redeemed."

"Or the House made of Magic Straw will collapse," Mom added.

Next: How the Ghost of the Wampum Makers Stole the Global Economy

Part 6: How the Wampum Makers' Ghost Stole the Global Economy

Mom and Dad Normal settled into their living room with a bowl of popcorn. Their daughter, Sue B. Normal would be home from her school teacher job soon. She and their son, Abe Normal, promised to explain to them how YouTube protected them from becoming wards of the state, in a global economic meltdown. They were eager to learn.

Sue B. set up her slide projector, and started her PowerPoint presentation, carefully recording her screen shots to make a video of her analysis.

The Web of Deceit Operating the Fractional Reserve System

The Ghost in the Machine, by Sue B. Normal

Now Henry Bankster, in 2008, was the main Bankster. His concern was the global network of the Cult of the Spoons, whose Witch Doctors pointed out to him that their wampum was missing from the hole, and it had never been paid back. They hadn't worried about that for the last 36 years, but now that Lehman Brothers, one of their own members, had gone bankrupt, they were making a big stink.

You see, as Head Bankster, Henry was in charge of making sure cash flowed, regardless of the underlying mechanisms. In this case, it was true that too many of the poor people had been given loans from the Banksters' Magic Straw. They were not making their payments to the Spoon Cartel. The Spoon Cartel was furious, and they demanded payment now, or they would take all their money back that they loaned to the United States of America six generations ago.

Henry knew that the only solution was to print lots and lots and lots more Magic Straw, so he could give it to the Cartel, to make up for the payments the poor people didn't make. He decided his best bet would be to take the American and British Tribal Chiefs into his *CON*-fidence.

"What should we tell the Poor People?" the American Chief asked. "They will think the new money we print is theirs. They will think it is tax money."

"I know it makes you sad to deceive them," said the Bankster. "I, too, am greatly saddened to deceive the poor people. But the money is truly not their tax money. It is newly printed money, in the form of more debt. When more money is printed, it devalues the currency, making their goods and services cost more. So their future will be rife with high costs for everything they buy. But they are very stupid and misinformed, so they will never find out. You could explain it clearly, but they do not like Math, so when you tell them, it will whoosh right over the top of their heads. They will never understand that this is all just new debt, new Magic Straw, and a wholly new Paradigm. They still think of wampum as being something physical, like GOLD. I don't think it's even possible to explain it clearly to such people as they are. We would be foolish to even try."

"But what about the Parliament," said the British Chief. "What will we tell the Parliament?"

"Here," said Henry Bankster. "Tell the Parliament we told the Congress this." Henry whipped out a piece of paper, three pages long, that said, "You give Henry Bankster $700 Billion RIGHT NOW, and don't you dare ask him what he's going to do with it. Signed, The Chief."

"But what if they tell you to go eat sh#t?" asked the British Chief.

"Then we do what Gangsters have always done," said Henry.

The American Chief nodded, as he explained, "We take them into the coat room, one at a time, and we tell them we're going to declare martial law if they don't do it."

"But what will the Poor People say?" asked the British Chief.

"Oh, don't worry about the Poor People," answered Henry. "As soon as we pay all the Spoons, we'll tell their Witch Doctors what happened. Then the Witch Doctors will go buy all the television stations in the world, and all the newspapers in the world, and they will tell the Poor People what to think."

"Great idea," said the American Chief. "Once all the television and newspapers are bought and paid for, we will no longer have to worry about the Poor People. Ever. We will feed them their opinions, all day, every day, on a 24 hour news cycle. They will stop threatening the Witch Doctors and the other Spoons forever."

"But . . . what about the Internet?" said the British Chief.

"The Internet?" said Henry Bankster. "I don't know much about this Internet. I'm an old man who doesn't interact with Poor People. Do they use the Internet?"

"Oh, my, yes," said both the Chiefs. "The Poor People love their pets, and their Internet. Pets and Internet are the two things they will keep, even when they are very poor."

"All right then. All right then," said Henry. He bit his nails and walked around the room in circles. "Can we turn the Internet off?"

"No!" shouted the Chiefs. "Even if we wanted to, it's gotten away from us. We couldn't shut it down if we tried."

Much to the Chiefs' surprise, Henry started vomiting, dry heaves, right there in the room in front of them. "I need to go on a ski vacation," Henry announced. "To calm my nerves. Here's my cell phone number at the most expensive Colorado resort on the planet. I'll handle the crisis from there. My friend Ken Lay, who actually did not die, but faked his death and is now living on a South Pacific Island sipping mai tais with Elvis, loaned me his ski mansion."

So the Bankster went on a ski vacation, and the Witch Doctors sent their bodyguards to the cloak room, to explain to the U S Congress what was going to happen next.

But all the Poor People of the Tribe didn't understand. By the time they recovered from the shock, the Witch Doctors had purchased all the television stations and all the newspapers, so nobody could tell them what happened.

And the Internet? Well, on the Internet, opinions are like @ssholes. Everybody has their own. The Poor People couldn't distinguish the Blueberry Pies from the PopTarts, so they looked away. The only record of what really happened was on a YouTube video. And it was hidden among hundreds of thousands of YouTube videos, most of which were horse puckey. So nobody ever knew, and the Banksters took their profits and invited the IRS to join them at a conference in Vegas. The IRS paid.

"Poor Henry Bankster," Mom added. "He was such a good man, and so misunderstood."

Next: What if we all bought gold?

Part 7: What if we all bought gold?

"That would solve it, wouldn't it" Dad asked.

"Solve what?" Said Sue.

"The U S Debt crisis. We wouldn't have to worry about inflation destroying our savings, if we all bought gold," answered Dad.

Sue's brother, Abe, heard this and added his own opinion. "I guess," Abe observed.

"When the electricity goes out, and the shelves in the stores are empty, your neighbor who owns chickens might agree to take a gold coin worth $1,800 for a few chicken eggs. But if that is the situation, your neighbor might demand something more practical as barter, like a box of nails, instead."

"It depends. We, the Normal Family,

Gold Coins: The Solution?

wouldn't have to worry about inflation destroying our savings, if we, the Normal Family, had our savings in physical gold. But that's physical gold, not a piece of paper that says we bought gold. And that assumes that only a small percentage of people do it, and that the economy is still operating so that we can exchange it for currency when we need it," Sue explained.

"Huh?" Dad offered.

Sue didn't know if she was up to this explanation. Maybe Henry Bankster was right. Maybe the Middle People didn't have the capacity to know the sinister trickery of the banking system. But, she'd committed to explaining this to Mom and Dad, so she kept going.

"First, Dad," she said, "everybody can't buy gold. That was the problem in the first place. Gold is a specific, limited physical object. There isn't enough of it to operate the world economy. The more people try to buy it, the more expensive it gets. That's why Nixon took America off the gold standard in the first place. Money outgrew the physical limitations of how much gold existed. It couldn't keep going up and up in value, because to inflate the value of the gold to that extent would destroy the fortunes of the original Spoon Cartel, who now had nothing left but Promissory Notes."

"Now I'm confused," interrupted Mom Normal, entering the living room and wiping her hands on her apron. "First, you tell me the reason we have so much debt is because we went off the gold standard. Now you're telling me we can't go back on it."

"Think about the Banker who has an empty hole, with no wampum in it," Sue told her. "Going back on the gold standard isn't going to put any wampum in it. It's just going to make all the dollars worthless, because they aren't based on gold. The only people with money would be the ones who owned physical gold. The United States Treasury would be completely empty then."

"That's ridiculous," Mom stated. "The United States could use its dollars to buy gold."

"No," Sue said. "Dollars wouldn't have any value. The only value in money is the perceived value. Until somebody agrees that money has value, it's silly play money. Monopoly money."

"Yeah?" Dad interrupted. "I don't believe you. Somebody should try it. Put us back on the gold standard."

"Actually," Abe contributed, "in history, there were two U.S. Presidents who tried to change the system of paper money, distributed by an independent banking system called the Federal Reserve. Each of these two Presidents realized that the Federal Reserve system created a fake debt to the Spoon Cartel. They understood that the Federal Reserve is not an arm of the government. It's an independent group of banks, who loan fake air-based money to the U.S. Treasury, printed out of thin air. Then they expect to be paid interest, which goes to the Spoon Cartel, rather than the American people. The Federal Reserve started out as Wampum Makers, loaning their money to the nation. But now, it's evolved into a criminal enterprise. It operates outside the government, independent of oversight, and for the benefit of only the Spoons. It requires Cash to grease its wheels, and so it makes a Shell Game, for drug money and gun running to launder through. Each of these two Presidents proposed an idea for the U.S. Treasury to issue its own money, backed by gold, that would not involve the group of independent Bankers called the Federal Reserve system. If the U.S. issued its own money, instead of borrowing the money from the Banksters and the Spoon Cartel, it would not have to pay interest to itself."

"Okay. Who were these two brave and forward-thinking Presidents, who proposed to solve the problem of the U S Treasury owing money to the Federal Reserve Bank, which is not a government-controlled entity?" asked Mom.

"Wait for it," said Abe. "Wait for it. The two American Presidents who proposed having the U.S. Treasury issue debt directly, without going through the independently-owned Federal Reserve Bank system were . . . "

Drum roll, please.

(Humpty Dumpty falling off the Wall Street.)

"Lincoln and Kennedy," Abe told her.

[THIS SECTION STILL REDACTED BY THE WARREN COMMISSION, EVEN FIFTY YEARS AFTER THE FACT.]

Next post: How high can the debt ceiling go?

Part 8: How High can the Debt Ceiling Go?

Dad Normal has done a lot of thinking about what Sue and Abe have taught him. He corners Sue at the breakfast table, where she is gathering up her books to get to her teaching job at the middle school.

"You know, Sue," said Dad. "I think you're right. The world can't go back on the gold standard. A few individuals can squirrel it away for a rainy day, as long as everybody doesn't do it. Those individuals will be better off than if they relied on a 401K plan at the office. But the world got a lot bigger, and there isn't enough physical gold to meet everybody's growing needs. Going back on the gold standard would mean world economic development came to a halt. The Chinese, Indian, and Third World people whose economies are expanding would not be able to grow. The gold standard won't work for the world economy any more. What's happening is that countries who don't want the United States to be the world's dominant power are considering a way to make a basket of currencies be the global reserve currency. The problem is that nobody's sure what would happen if they did that. What if China bought Russia's oil without using U S Dollars? What if China stopped buying U S Debt? What would happen to the value of China's currency? Nobody knows. So far, that uncertainty has been sufficient to keep too many people from doing it. The only thing that is certain is that there's no way for the nations to go back to the gold standard. The world has passed the point of no return on the wampum system. But what else can work better?"

DANGER
Electric
shock risk

"So do you think the global economic system could collapse?" Mom asked, as she inserted another Eggo into the toaster.

"The system depends on ever-expanding markets," Sue explained. "Like every Ponzi scheme, it has to keep growing to survive."

"Meaning, the U S Debt has to keep going up," Mom clarified. "But what happens if the U S Debt goes down?"

"The U S Debt is a measure of how many U S Dollars other countries are buying. So the only way for the U S Debt to go down is to expand U S Exports, or to contract U S Imports," Sue told her. "We can't expand exports, because we aren't building anything to sell. And if we contract imports, it means our people aren't buying anything, since everything we buy is made outside of America. So that means to make the debt go down, we have to collapse the U S Economy. And if the U S Economy collapses, the global savings of other countries is devalued."

"We have to keep exporting dollars, then, is what you're saying," Dad interrupted. "We have to keep expanding the debt, forever."

"Or at least for as long as whatever politician is currently in office expects to be re-elected. When we stop expanding the debt, the Ponzi scheme unravels. It's like Bernie Madoff. Everybody was happy investing their money with him. He paid big returns. And then one day too many people showed up at the Wampum Window, and Bernie was caught. The U.S. has to keep expanding the debt, until the day when too many members of the Spoon Cartel or the Pirate Nouveau Riche call their loans."

"You're saying that Congress is going to continue to expand the debt ceiling, every time the issue comes up?"

"Yes, and I'm also saying that Congress, or the CIA, or the President of the United States, or whomever it is that makes these decisions, is going to continue to go to war wherever the opportunity to prevent oil from being sold for some currency other than the U S Dollar, sticks its camel's nose under the tent."

"We're going to war for oil?"

"Nope. We're going to war for the relationship between the U.S. Dollar and the ability to purchase oil. Because the cost of not going to war would be greater than the cost of doing nothing. The cost of a collapse in the value of the dollar would be unthinkable. Globally. For all the countries whose reserves are in U.S. Dollars."

"Sue, that's enough," Mom insisted. "The President of the United States would never let us go to war for such an evil reason."

Abe raised his hand. "Uh, Mom?" he said. "I'm not really sure the CIA lets the President in on the reason."

"Well, now, that's true," Dad offered. "The Doctrine of Plausible Deniability allows the CIA to do things that the President never finds out about. Protecting the U S Dollar through acts of war and assassination would fall under that category."

https://en.wikipedia.org/wiki/Plausable_deniability

"Good grief," said Mom. "Now you're being completely ridiculous. I won't hear any more of this crazy conspiracy theory. But, I do see that increasing the U.S. Debt is not a sustainable practice. It has to end somewhere."

Next: Where can this all end?

Part 9: Where can this all end?

"What economic system is sustainable?" Mom Normal asks her daughter, Sue B. Normal.

"The world as a whole is sustainable." Sue answers. "If you look at history, what happens? Empires rise and fall in waves. Macedonia, China, Egypt, Greece, Rome, Great Britain, and now the United States. Empires rise, they display their power, and after a few hundred years, they fall. That's the sustainable world model. So now it's the USA's turn to fall. That's all that's happening here. Some other country will rise next. And then they will fall."

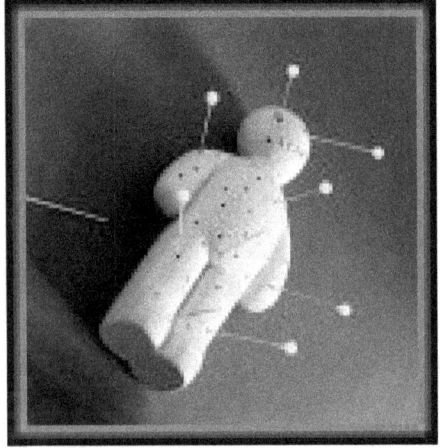

Voodoo Economics at work

"Whoa there, Daughter." Says Baby Boomer Dad. "The USA is the greatest country the world has ever seen. It's not an empire. It's a model for everyone to copy. The USA is not going to fall."

Abe breaks out in hysterical laughter.

Sue and Abe exchange looks. Sue smiles.

"Dad," she says softly. "The USA controls the currency used to buy oil, forcing every other country in the world to buy U S Dollars if they are going to buy oil to have electricity. No other country can grow unless it buys U S Dollars. As a result, the dollar is a strong currency in the world market. Other countries hold it as their reserve currency. Other countries hold the US Debt. But in the U.S., young people graduate from college with high debt, and no jobs. The Ponzi scheme of the Federal Reserve has no option but to keep increasing the debt of the United States of America, with no end. As the U S Debt increases, the Federal Reserve prints more money. As it prints more money, inflation goes up. Eventually, the purchasing power of the dollar in the U.S. will be too low for Americans to live comfortably. America becomes a Third World Country, and some other nation takes over the position of Empire."

" The income gap between rich and poor has increased so dramatically that the six members of the WalMart family have more income than the bottom 40% of the American people. And the WalMart family aren't even Spoons!" Abe added. "Top corporate CEOs make 400% of the average salary of their people. That's up from 40% when Reagan was President."

"Oh, I don't know. Inflation hasn't been so bad," Mom observed.

"How did we start this conversation?" said Sue. " In Part 1, you pointed out that your credit card bill today was 100% higher than it was five years ago, purchasing the same goods and services. That's 20% inflation per year in the last five years."

"But the government says inflation was only about 2% over the last five years," said Mom.

"Don't be ridiculous. Look at your bills. Gas for your car. Food at the grocery store. Rent. Health insurance. Your bills have gone up, but your wages have not. You know perfectly well that inflation has happened. The government changed the counting system, so you wouldn't know." Said Sue.

"You know what you are?" challenged Dad. *"You're a conspiracy theorist!"*

"If I am," said Sue, "then the toothpaste of Knowledge has squeezed out of my tube of Understanding. I can't stop knowing what I know."

"Me,too," said Abe. "Now that I understand the Evil Intention, how can I get a job and work for this Corporate Satan? What can my generation do, when we'll never have savings, never buy houses, never move out of our parents' basement? We have no hope!"

"He's right, George," Mom Normal said to Dad Normal. "If the new generations have no hope for a better future than their parents' had, our country is declining."

George Normal didn't answer his wife, Linda. He was busy counting his money, and emptying all the piggy banks in the house.

Next: Where is this Voodoo economic disaster leading our next generations?

Part 10. Where is this Voodoo economic disaster leading our next generations?

"So as we've explained," said Sue. "If nothing changes, the U S must remain in ever-increasing debt, to keep the Ponzi scheme from collapsing. That means more and more money has to be printed by the Federal Reserve. And what is the Federal Reserve? It's not an arm of government. It's a consortium of banks. The banks, at their core, are acting in the interest of the Spoon Cartel, who hold the original debt of the nation."

Piggy Banks got their name because . . .

"It's Foxes, who are busy guarding the hen house." Abe offered.

"Yes, it's the group of Witch Doctors and their Spoon Cartel, who owned all the wampum in the first place. They originally contributed to the U.S. Treasury, but that was generations ago, in the days of pirate ships and fledgling revolutionary governments. Is their interest in figuring out a way for the world to share equitably in their wampum?"

"Some would argue that it is. That we all hang together or we each hang separately. In the long term, capitalism at its best looks out for the interests of its consumers, as well as its wealth owners," said Mom.

"Sure," said Sue. "Some would argue that. But those who make that argument generally don't receive their invitation to the meeting of the Witch Doctors. So no, their concern isn't with making the world a better place. Their concern is keeping the Fox families well-fed, well-entertained, and well-endowed. So what do they do?"

"They set up a trade school across the bridge from Cambridge to teach future Henry Banksters to do a good job at guarding the family wealth," offered Dad.

"Yes, yes, they do that," Sue said. "But what else do they do?"

"They buy all the news media to make sure the public never understands economics," added Abe.

"Okay, yes, they do that, too. But what really, really important thing do they do, that ensures their future?" challenged Sue.

"They move their money into the debt of other nations, ahead of the dollar collapse, so they won't be hurt by it," guessed Mom.

"Bingo," said Sue.

http://blogs.wsj.com/wealth/2011/05/18/the-rich-are-moving-more-money-overseas/

"When the demand for the U S Dollar falls, U S Treasury Bond prices fall, which is doubletalk for interest rates rise. People become less able to pay their bills. Ultimately, the gap between rich and poor widens. It keeps widening, as unemployment rises. Eventually, the economy is so weakened it collapses. Money has so little value that people need wheelbarrows full of dollars, just to buy a loaf of bread."

"So what does a poor schmo like me do, to protect my family?" Asked Dad

"Assume the collapse is coming," said Sue. "Live like it's definitely on its way."

Next: How to prepare for the collapse of the global economy

Part 11: How to prepare for the collapse of the global economy

"Abe," said Sue, "Let's see if you can figure this out. It's about our generation. You and me. First, can the U S Government stop the Dollar from taking a big fall?"

Abe was ready. He'd studied all about this on the Internet. He was a YouTube aficionado. "They can postpone it," he said. "By continuing to raise the debt ceiling, and continuing to bully and threaten the oil-producing nations. They can threaten to bomb any country that makes plans to sell its oil in any denomination other than

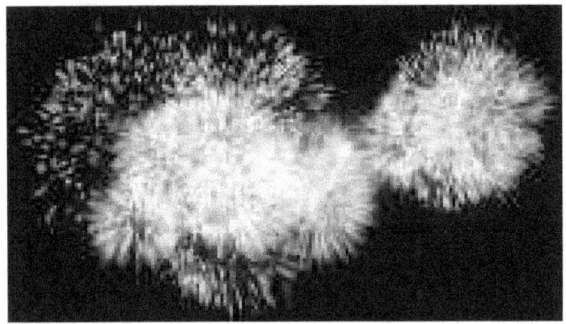

Fireworks are coming. It's not IF, it's WHEN.

U S Dollars, as they did with Iraq and Iran. They can threaten any country that tries to open up the oil market to competitive forces, as they did with Syria. But the world is losing patience with that, and although the Dollar's collapse can be postponed, it can't be averted."

Dad listened closely. "So the question isn't If, it's When," he inserted.

"Yes," answered Sue. "The question is When. Our response to it depends on how old we are. Young people, for example, who may not have much savings in U S Dollars, can be satisfied to be sure their future savings are in physical gold coins. Of course, you have to have possession of these gold coins. And you have to keep them safe, because Pirates could steal them and you couldn't get them back. I wouldn't put them in a safety deposit box at a bank, though. Who knows when the Pirates might grab that whole Bank thing and shake it until it vomits. It's a bit of a dilemma."

Mom popped out of her fear-induced coma to ask, "And older people? What can the Baby Boomers do?"

"Older people can move their savings into gold, if they have any savings," Sue offered. "But that brings us to the question of HOW this collapse might happen. If the collapse is a gradual decline in the value of the dollar, over a long time period, with the basic infrastructure of society locked in place, then gold is the answer. Gold will retain its value, or become more valuable, as the dollar declines. In small doses, an individual family can sell it to live. But if the collapse comes on suddenly, gold won't be the currency of value. Nails, food, water, bullets, fencing, and electricity will be the items of value."

"Oh, you mean like the Zombie Apocalypse?" said Abe.

"Right," said Sue, preparing to go out on a date. She was tiring of teaching these old people things. "If there's a shutdown in services, if there's a breakoff of the food distribution system, if there's a problem with the electric grid, then people will need the basics of life more than they will need gold. Gold can't feed you if you're isolated and alone. The only thing to do is arrange your life so that you have a sustainable society, a community like in colonial times, where one person knew how to shoe horses, and another person knew how to raise pigs."

"That's messed up," said Abe. He was beginning to get the shakes from being away from his video games for too long.

"I don't know, Abe," suggested Dad. "Maybe since you don't have a good job, you could take the lead in getting our family ready to live sustainably."

"No. No way. I'm busy. I have to update my Facebook page," Abe answered. Abe turned and ran out of the room.

Mom watched him go, and decided to pick up her knitting and sit in the living room. "We're not convinced, dear," she said over her shoulder, in good-bye to her daughter, Sue. "We don't believe it. We can't believe it. We won't believe it. It would be too hard."

"It would be very hard," said Sue. "I can see you need further convincing before you would embark on a path that would change your lives. Perhaps you would believe it if you saw it on Mainstream News."

CBS News Admits FEMA Camps are Real
http://thecommonsenseshow.com/2012/11/12/cbs-news-admits-fema-camps-are-real/

"Why do we need FEMA Camps?" Sue asked her dad, who was the only person left standing in the room.

Next: What can Mom and Dad Normal do to protect their family from the FEMA Camps?

Part 12: What can Mom and Dad Normal do to protect their family from the FEMA Camps?

Sue B. Normal pulled out her flipcharts again. It was a new day. Dad had convinced Mom and Abe to come back to the dining room and listen to Sue. She showed the family her outline plan to get them prepared for the collapse of the global economy. She said, "Here are some of the things we, as a family, would have to consider if we wanted to prepare for the collapse of the US economy."

Living Sustainably on the Farm

Tales from the Zombie Apocalypse

Table of Contents to:

A Handbook for Living in a Post-Consumer World

1. Look out for the Zombies: Scenarios for America's Future
2. Shelter: heating, sleeping arrangements, money and budgets
3. Water
4. Transportation
5. Communication and Community
6. Energy: gas, oil, solar, wind
7. Self-defense
8. Storing, growing, and procuring food
9. Hunting and fishing
10. Sourcing meats
11. Pantry storage
12. Gardening
13. Saving seeds
14. Composting

15. Canning
16. Dehydrating
17. Vacuum packing and freezing
18. Root cellaring
19. Smoking and butchering
20. Cooking
21. Raising chickens
22. Raising a dairy cow
23. Cleaning and laundry
24. First aid and medicines
25. Choosing a job for a village economy
26. Village money: local currency and finding your tribe
27. Relationships and stress relief
28. Finding the silver lining

"Holy Mind-blow, Batman," said Abe. "That is too far out. Too much. Not possible. Can't do it."

"You know, Dear," Mom said to Sue, "we don't even believe you. You're a conspiracy theorist. The United States of America is Exceptional. We don't have to be worried about these things."

"Absolutely, Sue," added Dad. "You've got to settle down and find a husband. You're going too far over the edge with these conspiracy theories."

"Okay, folks. I know how you feel," said Sue. "It would be pretty awful to have to change the way we live. I guess you're right. We should ignore all this stuff about the Spoon Cartel, and the NSA Spying, and the FEMA Camps, and the Homeland Security drones preparing for martial law. We should just wait until it happens, and then line up to get on the buses to take us to the Holding Cages. I mean, the FEMA Camps. We can trust the government to protect us from ourselves. You're right. It's too hard to do anything else."

"Damn straight," said Abe. He pulled out his iphone and started texting.

"You know what I'm going to do," said Dad, getting up from his chair and smiling happily. "I'm going to forget all about this and go read a book."

"Perfect idea" said Mom. "I'll read it, too. What should we read?"

"I have a suggestion," offered Sue. "Why don't we all read *The Tempest Illusion, by F T Moore?*"

"That's not an economics book is it?" Dad asked.

"No," Sue laughed. "It's a thriller. Fun reading. It will take your mind off heavy stuff like the Federal Reserve bank and the Spoon Cartel. It's all about how the CIA works for the Spoon Cartel instead of the Tribal Chief."

"Nothing in it about the Assassination Teams that roamed South America and killed despots?"

"No, no. Not a word about the Middle East, or the Russian gas pipelines. Nothing whatever about the Saudi King who went into a coma, lost all his vital organs, and then mysteriously came back to life and was quoted giving advice about Egypt."

"Nothing at all about the Syrian chemical weapons that came from Libya via the Benghazi CIA Station?"

"Nada," said Sue. "Although it does bring up the drone technology criss-crossing America's heartland. Nothing about the SWAT teams shooting tourists in the American police state. Not one single word about Monsanto poisoning the food supply. And do you know why it has nothing in it about these things?"

"Because it's FICTION!" shouted Abe.

"And all those things," Mom muttered, tears welling up in her eyes.

"Are not fiction," finished Dad.

Next: What to do if you can't stand to think about Truth

The Tempest Illusion
A Political Thriller
By F T Moore

"Because some Truths can only be told through fiction"

Chapter 1
Along the Southwestern Border of Guatemala:
A Shadowy Time in the Past

The assassin lay motionless in the thick, wet foliage, teasing the edge of the eighty-foot cliff, his eyes hanging over the treacherous drop. Dripping with unattended sweat, his eyebrows yielded and his eyes blurred. He wiped them with his camouflage shirt sleeve, slowly, carefully, not wanting to reveal his position with body movement. Waiting. He waited, while every breath pumped heated air into his already-simmering lungs, building to a near-suffocation. Panting, he struggled to circulate air. His breath resonated, a bong in his teetering mind, drowning out the piercing shrieks of jungle macaws. He feared exposure from his breathing huff or his warrior scent. His muscles ached from the tension of keeping still. After four days in this bug-infested furnace, the dampness had irritated the old injury in his right knee. Pain, alternating between a dull throb and a crippling stab, sliced from his shinbone to his thigh. He judged himself able to complete his task, but he knew he must finish today, before the knee swelled.

He worked at risk now. Stupidly. He regretted his agreement to come out alone, with no one to cover his back while he focused on the job. Momentarily, his mind strayed to admonish himself for accepting the terms they had offered. With the training of a professional, he suppressed his thought. Motionless work required motionless mind. Longer and longer, he waited, like a jungle cat, stalking his prey.

From the low morning position of the sun, he knew he had less than an hour before the cargo plane passed by on its scheduled humanitarian supply run. Today's plane would be his last chance. Today, he would do his job and get out. Fighting against the pain, he concentrated on removing his mind from his senses, ignoring the sweltering heat and tickling ants climbing his neck. Summoning the discipline of his training, he waited and waited again.

At last he saw shadows in the tent entrance. When the balding head and the heavy frame of his target appeared, he squinted through the powerful, wide angle scope of his surgically precise Remington M40A1. Locking the site onto the shaded flap in front of the tent, he steadied his arm, his body, and his mind, and the rifle steadied with him. Rhythmically, he settled his breathing into a natural pattern. Slowly, in timed cycle with his patterned breath, he squeezed the sensitive trigger.

The target's head exploded, splattering bones and brains. As the commander crumpled, the assassin scrambled to his feet, plunging away from the cliff through dense brush. The adrenaline of tribal war pushed him forward, forcing his strained body and throbbing leg to race along the pre-arranged path to his meeting place. Flipping the top of his hand-held radio, he entered the key code which would signal his rescuers. Limping, he made his way to the agreed-upon coordinates. Focusing, he directed his mind to the task of escape, allowing his thoughts no leeway to consider alternatives. Entertaining only the thought of his ultimate goal, he plowed unwaveringly forward. Stepping into the clearing at the pre-determined spot, he released a helium balloon. In response, the cargo plane, marked prominently with the logo of humanitarian aid and supplies for the peaceful citizens, extended a rope with a hook. Catching the balloon and the assassin in one swoop, the rope raised the assassin, dangling and twisting, into its cargo bay.

As he neared safety, the pressure of the last four days lifted. The mental block he had raised to protect his sanity dissolved. With its dissolution, his resistance fell. The pain in his knee kaleidoscoped knife-sharp agony through his body. His mind whirled with the concentrated stream of unanswered puzzles. The last words he heard before losing consciousness were the words of the pilot, sending the extraction radio code.

He was safe, in the hands of the homeland, with his good ole' friends.

The California mountains, north of Malibu
1996: A Time unlike Today

Chauncey Harrington Kiernan --- Chance, as he was called --- pulled on his jogging shoes and re-wrapped the bandage he wore continually around his right knee. The sun peered over the hills of his ranch in the rolling canyons of the California coast, halfway between Malibu and the Point Mugu Naval Base. Steep rolling ravines ended in holes and shadows, rather than curving valleys. Multiple shades of yellow, red, and brown shrubs twisted over the flowing hills. In the distance, trees grew in mutant shapes, mixing palms with distorted bushes, quiltwork patches of forest green among the shades of yellow. Above, the sunny blue sky broke only for the ominous wingspan of a condor, gliding from hilltop to hilltop, searching for prey. Chance had chosen the highest point on the hill for his homesite, providing a glimpse of the crashing ocean in the distance. He had built the house with his own hands, modeling it after a Western -style log cabin. Chance Kiernan wasn't you and he wasn't me. He was a different species, not like us. He didn't have the same feelings we have. He was more connected to the Earth than we are; a species suspended between animal and demi-god. Whatever humanity had been in him had been trained and sifted out.

Chance resigned from the military after his mission in Honduras. He had attained the rank of Lt. Colonel, through field operations in the Special Forces. Joint Special Operations Command, now, but Delta Force, then. He lived alone here on the ranch, but hired Marin, a Bolivian immigrant, to work with him every day. Marin lived in the bunker behind the main house, along with other ranch hands that Marin hired from time to time. Although Chance had undergone three operations on his leg, and years of physical therapy, he still walked with a limp. It annoyed him, to be less than perfect.

It was barely dawn. Chance jogged, as best he could while favoring his injured leg, the quarter mile to the edge of his land. He climbed his homemade obstacle course, lifting weights, stretching every muscle in his body. He enjoyed physical experience. He believed it to be communion with the Earth. He loved the thrill of feeling his senses. The sun burned off the morning haze, and Chance arrived at his target range. Chance considered his target shooting to be mental therapy. He used shooting to focus his mind, concentrating his intensity. When he focused his mind on form, aim, and skill, he knew he could keep his mind from racing into memories he didn't want to recall. Whenever he felt tense, he returned to his shooting range

47

to release energy, to focus his mental power. Only after his business of exercise and shooting was complete would he return to the cabin to prepare his breakfast. The life of a hermit suited him, and he expected that he would be alone forever.

It was mid-morning before he returned to the yard to begin the day's work, steaming coffee in hand. Marin dragged the sheep they would slaughter into the work area. With a skilled strike, Chance slit its throat. Just then, the flock of geese Chance kept as pets honked a warning alarm. He dropped his bloody knife on the ground by the sheep's carcass. Wiping his hands on his worn jeans, he got up off his knees. Reaching inside the screen door, he pulled his revolver out of its leather holster hanging behind the kitchen door; he inserted the gun, muzzle down, inside the back of his waistband. Hugging the wall, he tread slowly around the outside of the wood cabin to the front yard.

Joe Bridgewell crouched inside his rental car, parked halfway down the mud driveway where a large dog-sized gander lowered its neck in attack posture, squawking a threat. Joe's eyes revealed the fear of the cornered.

"Normal people have dogs," he yelled at Chance through the cracked open car window.

Chance smiled as he sauntered across the barren patch of land. Two black labrador puppies barreled out the screen door, yapping at the gander.

"I have dogs," Chance responded.

As Joe timidly opened the car door, the gander ran away, honking and flapping. Joe brushed the dust off his vested blue suit.

"You know," he said, "if you got a phone, I wouldn't have to fly three thousand miles to talk. Who doesn't have a phone, buddy? I can tell you the Avis people are going to have a fit when they see what that so-called road you built did to their Camaro." Joe's Boston accent hadn't softened in fifteen years of life in Washington, D.C. His military-cut blond hair and tall, angular body fit perfectly in a three piece suit and wingtips.

Chance, dressed in cowboy boots and a plaid flannel shirt, looked every bit the refugee from an old Western movie. His reddish-brown hair cut a shade longer than Joe's, but its thickness gave Chance a boyish look. With his trace of freckles, Chance, at thirty-eight, still left the impression he could, at any time, play a silly prank. "I have a phone," he said to his friend. "It's in the refrigerator. Keeps it from geo-locating when I'm not using it."

Joe's mind was still recovering from the drive up Decker Canyon Road, a daredevil experience of hairpin turns, steep inclines, and narrow edges, along a ledge that dropped straight down a crashing ravine. The road seemed more suited to donkey travel than a six-cylinder engine. Even the air in this place bespoke a place separated from the chill of the East Coast Joe had left behind only hours before.

Joe appeared disoriented to Chance, disturbed in a way that did not gel.

If it don't gel, it ain't Jello, Chance thought to himself. Words he lived by. The mantra of an assassin, staying alive by knowing the signs. His friend needed a beer, Chance decided. He looked at the low morning sun. *Hell, it's past noon somewhere,* he thought, as he returned to the cabin's kitchen and brought out a six pack.

"Take this with you while you change your clothes," he said as he handed Joe a Killian's Irish Red ale. "We got a lot of catching up to do."

Twenty years ago, when they began as trainees in Delta Force, Joe and Chance never imagined they would someday be employer and agent. They'd been soldiers then, and they remained soldiers together for eight years. But, times had changed. Now Joe Bridgewell worked for the government agency which was in times past called the Intelligence Support Activity, a division of Army Intelligence. At least, that's what his paycheck once said, although the changing names on the issuing side may have confused an outsider. Chance Kiernan worked for himself, a private citizen, who took a contract occasionally from a trusted friend. Regardless of the name of their employers, both knew they were the good guys. Both knew their intentions and motivations lived on the side of the law. Both knew, on the inside, they worked for the love of life. On the record books, some called them killers. On the book as they read it, they were guardians of life. Patriots, they considered themselves. Patriots to the concept of the United States of America. Loyal sons of the Homeland, who had stalwartly defended it with their lives.

Joe and Chance sat together outside on the sandy ground, sharing the six-pack. It was a brilliant, sunny day, but they could see rainclouds forming at the edge of the mountaintops.

"We've come a long way since Delta, buddy," Joe said. The words flashed a picture of fire in a desert sandstorm at night. Too many scenes of fires flashed through Chance's mind. He blocked the memories. Chance remained silent.

"We're opening up a HUMINT opportunity," Joe said, biting the end off a cigar he'd just pulled out of his shirt pocket. He reached into the same pocket and offered one to Chance. Chance took it, settled back to fiddle with it, avoided responding to Joe's bait. HUMINT meant Human Intelligence. It was the part of spying that carried the danger. Chance loved this life. He enjoyed risk. He breathed for danger.

"When I learned about it," Joe continued, "this HUMINT opportunity, I knew it was meant for you to do. I can't see anyone else being up to it."

Chance wasn't talking. He believed in the power of silence. He continued to puff the cigar and sip the beer. Eventually, Joe would spit the whole story out.

"Anyhow," Joe continued, as Chance predicted he would, to fill the void of silence, "this is a top level assignment. You'd have guys under you. They'd do . . ."

"I don't teach. I don't supervise. I don't babysit," Chance interrupted. "When I work, I work alone. I do what has to be done. I walk away."

"Yeah, I know," Joe responded. " Just humor me and hear me out, okay? Times are changing. Life is changing. War is changing. We're getting old, pal, you and me. But we're the experience to draw on. This is a hard nut to crack. We can't leave the young guys to make their mistakes on their own. HUMINT went nearly dormant for too many years. They need us, to train and advise the next wave. The training's been neglected. The young guys aren't ready."

Chance puffed. Then he swigged. Joe mirrored his actions.

"It's more than an attack of anthrax, or a hijacked plane, or a bombed building. It's more than tribal warfare, " Joe said. "It's bigger than the interests of the U.S., or its commerce."

Chance felt a chill travel down the base of his spine. He'd heard Joe say this before. He hadn't listened that time. In fact, he'd left the Army when he'd heard it. *Paranoia*, he thought, when Joe started down this road. Then, at a time of the height of Joe's warnings, Chance was caught in a fire set to burn his house down. The fire was meant to kill Chance, but he escaped. He had serious burns, and spent months in the hospital. After that, he left the Army, and he moved out here. Years passed before he took a contract again. No explanation was ever presented for the arson at his house. No leads panned out. No criminals were found, no blame placed. For years, Chance searched for the answer, agonized over the framing of the question. The burns on his chest healed, but for a time, he almost lost his mind. The work saved him. When he worked, he could direct his anger, imagine he was getting his revenge. Maybe he would pursue Joe's thinking now.

"What is bigger than the interests of U.S. commerce, meinKampf?" he asked Joe, blowing cigar smoke symbolically in Joe's direction. "Nothing's bigger than the interests of U.S. commerce."

"The discovery of a code, my friend," Joe answered, setting his beer can on the sandy ground beside him. He pulled himself up to be even with Chance's eyes. "A code inserted on the authority of the highest levels of U.S. government. A code working against U.S. interests. A code with its finger on the trigger of our nuclear options, and the power to direct our forces in the wrong direction. A code that is right now in the hands of those who must not be allowed to handle it. A destiny code, we've called it."

Chance shook his head. "Not buyin' it," he said. He spat on the ground. "Politics. I don't do 'em."

"Then I'll give you a more concrete example," Joe said. "A code, planted in an electronic circuit. A transfer of a technology that allows our armed drones to be re-directed, to have their controls over-ridden. A code in a chip that scrambles our direction, re-assembles our databases, and confuses our communications. And the person with access to plant the code, is your target on this mission."

Chance closed his eyes, rested his head back on the log wall. Flies buzzed around his knee, as he remembered the years of recovery. He felt the pressure to jump back in, take care of the problem, get control.

Chance knew some things about codes that few others knew. He knew things about human behavior that few others knew. He knew a few things even *he* wished he didn't know. Unconsciously, he ground his teeth. Chance Kiernan did not want to know what Joe Bridgewell came here to tell him. He dropped his head into his hands.

"Tell me everything," he growled.

Buy the Tempest Illusion now

www.FTMoore.com

The DawnFire Saga by F T Moore.

The U.S. Army trained him as an assassin. His women taught him the dangers of a world painted gray. Now he's our only hope for a new beginning. In a world filled with terror, can freedom be regained? Follow Chance Kiernan, from Delta Force to renegade patriot, in the DawnFire Saga by F.T. Moore.

The Tempest Illusion: Book One in the DawnFire Saga. When Chance Kiernan, assassin for hire, meets a young business woman on her first international assignment, the hard shell he constructed to save his own soul cracks. Katie Black is accused of spying, but when this hard- line soldier comes for her, she shows him a world of nuance where life and values are not black and white. The soldier pulls the lady out of the fire, but her fierce independence pushes both of them over the ledge. When Kiernan and Black get together, the gray areas of spy-vs-mercenary explode into a penetrating landscape of breadth and color. But tragedy seeks-and-destroys Kiernan's new world-view like a predator drone. His new wife and his twin sons become the anchor that drags this military predator down.

When our home-grown trained killers slip off their leashes, where might they go for revenge?

Copper Hollow: Book Two in the DawnFire Saga. Drinking 'shine, cheering at the chicken fights, loving their women, hunting squirrels. Life in the mountains. Until the drones circled overhead, the men, women, and children of Copper Hollow didn't know they were terrorists. Didn't know they had something to hide. Luke Trout graduated from high school and joined the Marines. Headed to Afghanistan to fight him some Taliban. Chance Kiernan, ex-Delta Force, headed to Copper Hollow to find peace. But peace wasn't waiting.

Copper Hollow is a hotbed of Intelligence Agency activity, and it's not only the CIA. This isolated area in the hollows of the Blue Ridge Mountains is the hideout of Te, a rogue mercenary agency, funding the Afghan insurgents. Manufacturing heroin from the poppy fields of Afghanistan, the rogue agency conceals its activity in empty chicken houses and backwoods sheds. But can Defense Intelligence Agent Chance Kiernan and his FBI Agent sidekick, Juliette March, uncover the operation before more citizens of Copper Hollow die? Or is the rogue agency not really so rogue?

A story so gripping and vivid you'll check the skies for the buzzing of drones overhead. May we never wake up to find that our home towns have become Copper Hollow.

Virgin of the DawnFire: Book Three in the DawnFire Saga. In the early dawn, two Haitian men arrive at the airport in Curacao. They are carrying the potion to make a zombie out of the evil and dark Josh Bockenheim. Stopped at the airport, they make a call to their high priestess. The exotic and beautiful Brigitte Arceneaux is both a voodoo priestess and a doctor of biomedicine in Haiti. But the failure to stop Bockenheim's plot sets off a cascade of events which collapse the world's economy. Martial law is declared in America, and the starving citizens line up to ride buses to FEMA refugee camps. As the citizens of the world respond to the chain of disasters triggered by Bockenheim's plan, it is up to Arceneaux and Chance Kiernan together to renew the world order. But can their ragged band of patriots, living a primitive life in the back woods, overcome the forces of corruption and greed that have overtaken the American government? Can these two male and female former assassins bring a new dawn to the beleaguered and imprisoned citizens of the USA, and reignite the fire of American democracy?

Covering thirty years of American life and global commerce, the DawnFire Saga turns conspiracy theory on its head. A story that will change your outlook on America, and chill you to the marrow of your bone.

 Published by Pergados Press

About the Author

 F T Moore is a former software developer who worked for multiple defense contractors over thirty years. After writing the DawnFire Saga, Moore is hiding in the hills. Moore is the author of the political satire: *Packing for FEMA Camp* and blogs about life in America

Author of the DawnFire Saga

The U.S. Army trained him as an assassin. His women taught him the dangers of a world painted gray. Now he's our only hope for a new beginning. In a world filled with terror, can freedom be regained? Follow Chance Kiernan, from Delta Force to renegade patriot, in the *DawnFire Saga* by F.T. Moore.

Blog: AuthorFTMoore.wordpress.com

Follow F T Moore on Twitter @FTMoore1

Find more books by F T Moore at:

www.FTMoore.com

Read more Mom and Dad Normal on
FT Moore's blog:

AuthorFTMoore.wordpress.com

(And find out what happens when Abe Normal mines for
Bitcoin.)